The Weight of Ants

The Weight of Ants

By David Paquet
Translated by Leanna Brodie

Scirocco Drama

The Weight of Ants
Original title: *Le poids des fourmis*
first published 2023 by Scirocco Drama
An imprint of J. Gordon Shillingford Publishing Inc.

Scirocco Drama Editor: Glenda MacFarlane
Cover design by Doowah Design
Photo of David Paquet by Julie Artacho.
Photo of Leanna Brodie by Kristine Cofsky.
Production photos by Yanick Macdonald

Printed and bound in Canada on 100% post-consumer recycled paper.

Production Inquiries:

Agent for Leanna Brodie:
Michael Petrasek, Kensington Literary Representation
34 St. Andrew Street
Toronto, ON, Canada M5T 1K6
(416) 848-9648
kensingtonlit@rogers.com

Agent for David Paquet:
Corinne Giguère, Agence Artistique Corinne Giguère
2025A rue Masson, #101J
Montreal, QC H2H 2P7
514-379-1719 or 514-660-5158
info@agencecg.com

Library and Archives Canada Cataloguing in Publication

Title: The weight of ants / by David Paquet ; translated by Leanna Brodie.
Other titles: Poids des fourmis. English
Names: Paquet, David, 1978- author. | Brodie, Leanna, translator.
Description: A play. | Translation of: Le poids des fourmis.
Identifiers: Canadiana (print) 20230561128 | Canadiana (ebook) 20230561144 | ISBN 9781990738289 (softcover) | ISBN 9781990738395 (EPUB)
Classification: LCC PS8631.A666 P6413 2023 | DDC C842/.6—dc23

We acknowledge the financial support of the Canada Council for the Arts, the Government of Canada, the Manitoba Arts Council, and the Manitoba Government for our publishing program.

Canada Council for the Arts Conseil des arts du Canada Funded by the Government of Canada Canada Manitoba Arts Council Conseil des arts du Manitoba Manitoba

J. Gordon Shillingford Publishing
P.O. Box 86, RPO Corydon Avenue, Winnipeg, MB Canada R3M 3S3

David Paquet

David Paquet is a graduate in playwriting from the National Theatre School of Canada (2006) and lives in Montreal. His plays *Porc-épic, 2h14, Appels entrants illimités, Les grands-mères mortes* (co-written with Karine Sauvé), *Le brasier, Histoires à plumes et à poils* (co-written with Marie-Hélène Larose-Truchon and Érika Tremblay-Roy), *Le soulier, Chansons pour le musée* (co-written with Karine Sauvé), *Le poids des fourmis, L'éveil du printemps* (a reimagining of *Spring Awakening*), and *Papiers mâchés* and *Le Voilier (manifeste du fragile)* – two one-man-shows of stand-up poetry he performs himself – have gathered international praise and have been produced in more than a dozen countries all over North America and Europe. Paquet's work has won the Governor General's Literary Award for French-language drama (twice), the Prix Michel-Tremblay, the Prix Sony-Labou-Tansi (twice), the Québec Critic's Choice Award for TYA (twice), the Théâtre d'Aujourd'hui Audience Choice Award, a Jessie Richardson Award, and a Dora Mavor Moore Award. David Paquet also teaches playwriting for, among others, the National Theatre School of Canada, the Centre des auteurs dramatiques (CEAD), and the Conservatoire d'art dramatique de Montréal.

Leanna Brodie

Leanna Brodie is a leading translator of contemporary Québécois and Franco-Canadian playwrights. Recent productions have included David Paquet's *Wildfire* (Factory Theatre, Toronto: 2022 Dora Mavor Moore Award for Best New Play, Director, and Production); Joe Jack et John's *Violette* (Espace Libre/PuSh Festival); Mohsen El Gharbi's *Omi Mouna* (Impact Festival/Infinithéâtre); Anaïs Pellin's *Clementine* (Carousel Theatre/PHT, Vancouver); Fanny Britt's *Benevolence* (Ruby Slippers Theatre/Pacific Theatre); and Rébecca Déraspe's *I Am William* (Stratford Festival and Théâtre le Clou). She is also an award-winning playwright and actor whose work has been performed internationally. Brodie most recently served as Assistant Professor (Playwriting) at UBC's School of Creative Writing. *Salesman in China,* which she is co-writing with Jovanni Sy, will premiere at the Stratford Festival in 2024.
www.leannabrodie.com

Acknowledgements

The author would like to thank Mario Borges and Joachim Tanguay, the co-artistic and managing directors of Théâtre Bluff, for commissioning the play and offering him exactly what he needed: time and trust.

Playwright's Note

If you ask me, authors are sponges and sculptors: they soak up reality and sculpt it into fiction. In my previous play *Le soulier [The Shoe]*, I turned my attention to mental health; more specifically, to the courage of those who suffer and the humanity of those who help them keep their footing. After this incursion into the heart of our invisible wounds, I wanted to turn my gaze towards the tangible and the collective. *The Weight of Ants* would be more political than psychological. This time the concerned citizen, rather than the fragile individual, would shape the text.

I started reading, questioning, researching. Soon the sponge was swamped: political disillusionment and ambient cynicism; eco-anxiety and environmental crisis; apathy and citizen mobilization; personal gain versus collective good; corruption and abuse of power. A harsh study from which emerged a central question: what is it, today, to be young and to receive a battered Earth as a gift? How does one keep hope alive when "Happy Birthday" has been replaced by "Happy Doomsday"?

In response to this challenge, the sculptor has opted for political satire. Everything is exaggerated to the extreme. An ideal way, it seems to me, to offer a critique and yet avoid hammering the viewers with a message whose gravity they already know. Laughter and reflection are not incompatible. On the contrary: humour allows us to relax and digest what would otherwise be difficult to swallow.

Yes, *The Weight of Ants* is an x-ray of our collective anxieties, an inventory of the threats we face. Above all, however, the play is intended as a restorative ceasefire, especially for young people who find themselves confronted with problems that they absolutely did not cause. The idea is not to close our eyes to an uncertain horizon. On the contrary: it's an invitation to all of us to look in the same direction at the same time. *The Weight of Ants* is a reminder that when we act together, everything becomes not only lighter to carry, but also easier to shift. To transform.

– David Paquet, October 2019

Translator's Note

In *The Weight of Ants,* I have used "crap" and "BS" for words that could also be translated as "sh*t" and "bullsh*t." This was a judgment call about authorial intention, character, and situation. If you are staging the play in a context where the stronger versions seem funnier and more authentic and will not derail the entire performance, then by all means you may make those particular substitutions throughout.

Production History

Le poids des fourmis premiered in Montreal on November 19, 2019 in the Salle Fred-Barry at Théâtre Denise-Pelletier, in a Théâtre Bluff production directed by Philippe Cyr.

Cast:

JEANNE .... Élisabeth Smith

OLIVIER .... Gabriel Szabo

ALL THE REST .... Nathalie Claude and Gaétan Nadeau

Creative Team:

Assistant Director .... Vanessa Beaupré

Set Designer .... Odile Gamache

Costume Designer .... Étienne René-Contant

Lighting Designer .... Cédric Delorme-Bouchard

Sound Designer .... Christophe Lamarche-Ledoux

Production Manager .... Émanuelle Kirouac-Sanche

Technical Director .... Mélissa Perron

Photographs of the 2019 Théâtre Bluff production of *Le poids des fourmis* directed by Philippe Cyr.

Élisabeth Smith as Joan. Photo by Yanick Macdonald.

Gabriel Szabo as Olivier. Photo by Yanick Macdonald.

Gaétan Nadeau, Gabriel Szabo, Nathalie Claude. Photo by Yanick Macdonald.

Gaétan Nadeau, Élisabeth Smith. Photo by Yanick Macdonald.

Gabriel Szabo, Nathalie Claude. Photo by Yanick Macdonald.

Élisabeth Smith. Photo by Yanick Macdonald.

Élisabeth Smith, Gaétan Nadeau, Gabriel Szabo, Nathalie Claude.
Photo by Yanick Macdonald.

Élisabeth Smith, Gabriel Szabo. Photo by Yanick Macdonald.

Characters

Joan
Olivier
The Principal
Bertha from the Cafeteria
Emilio Who Teaches Too Many Subjects at the Same Time
Katie-Sue the Math Teacher
The Shampoo Ad
Olivier's Mother
The Woman Who Sells Books While Drunk
The Mayor
The Grocery Store Cashier
The Woman Who Drives the School Bus
Gabriella
Nort
Joey
The Psychologist
Mike
The Janitor
The Bookstore Owner
The Therapist
Raoul

Offstage Voices (or not):

The Man in a Suit and Tie

The Withered Old Woman

The Voice of the One Who Is Thirsty

The Voice of the One Who Is Hungry

The Voice of the One Who Is Hot

The Voice of the One Who Is Hurting

The Entire School

A Whirlwind of Voices

Someone in the Crowd

The Control Tower of Heaven

Someone Else in the Crowd

The play can be performed by four or more actors. Each company is free to distribute the roles as it sees fit.

Monday – The Candidates

Scene 1: Screw You, I'm Already Beautiful

THE PRINCIPAL:
(On the intercom.) Hello. This is your principal speaking. Stop booing, I don't like you either. As you know, last year we were ranked among the bottom 10 schools in the country. In other words, we're a bunch of losers. The good news: I'm retiring next year, so I don't care. The other good news: thanks to that list, we've received a special grant to help develop your blah-blah-blah… Which is why, today, we are proud to bring you the official launch of – *(Sound of a cheesy party horn.)* "Future Week." Basically, we're holding school elections to make you think you have power. Next, we'll throw a theme party to make you forget you have none. Excited? Me neither. Have a nice day.

JOAN:
(To the audience.) A crap medal. That's what my school deserves. Not a gold medal. Or a silver medal. Or bronze. A MEDAL OF CRAP. *(Calming down.)* Sorry: I try not to yell, but I can't help it... I call them my "Rage-O-Ramas", and I don't know why THEY ONLY HAPPEN TO ME... When you go to a school this bad, I think you've got to scream your head off... How did we end up here? Easy: our whole staff is just as inspiring as our principal. Take Bertha from the Cafeteria.

BERTHA FROM THE CAFETERIA:
Here ya go: lasagna.

JOAN:
There's no cheese. Or noodles.

BERTHA FROM THE CAFETERIA:
It's a three-layer lasagna: sauce, sauce, and sauce. Next.

JOAN:
Emilio teaches Music, History, Geography, Phys. Ed., and Science. He's not too thrilled about the cuts to education…

EMILIO WHO TEACHES TOO MANY SUBJECTS AT THE SAME TIME:
(Weeping.) Do re mi fa fa fa –

JOAN:
Burnout! Too bad: I loved his science class. Why? Because we learn how to blow things up, and it can be useful to know how to blow things up. But out of all of our teachers, the worst is the one who's standing in front of me right now: my math teacher, Katie-Sue...

KATIE-SUE THE MATH TEACHER:
Hello my little goobitty-goos! Today you'll not only learn how to count… You'll learn how to count on me!

JOAN:
She's a former kindergarten teacher who talks to us like we had a lobotomy.

KATIE-SUE THE MATH TEACHER:
Who'd like to sing the Pythagoras song with me?
Oh, this triangle has a right angle
So there's a lot to untangle
Take the square of every side –

JOAN:
Two options: turn her face into a right-angle triangle, or go to the washroom. I choose Option #2. I don't ask permission: I walk out of the classroom and head slowly down the hall. As soon as I'm in the toilet stall, I come face-to-face with an ad. An ad that looks me right in the eye –

THE SHAMPOO AD:
Hey, Joan! Wanna shampoo that makes you beautiful?

The SHAMPOO AD applies shampoo and approaches orgasm.

JOAN:
Gross...

THE SHAMPOO AD:
Or would you rather buy gum that makes you beautiful?

The SHAMPOO AD chews gum and approaches orgasm.

JOAN:
Are you an ad, or a porno?

THE SHAMPOO AD:
I'm only trying to help. I bet it's not easy, right?

JOAN:
What?

THE SHAMPOO AD:
Being ugly. Your face makes me want to call 911.

JOAN:
Who asked you?!

THE SHAMPOO AD:
Why don't you bring your neck to school? I think you'd be prettier with a neck.

JOAN:
SHUT UP.

THE SHAMPOO AD:
Hey, how about some lipstick? It might distract us from that massive overbite.

The SHAMPOO AD applies lipstick and approaches orgasm.

JOAN:
I take out a Sharpie and get to work... just as a janitor walks in. Ten minutes later, I'm in the principal's office.

THE PRINCIPAL:
So, *(Consulting a file.)* Joan... You vandalized a shampoo ad.

JOAN:
I didn't vandalize an ad: I vandalized THE ENTIRE SYSTEM.

THE PRINCIPAL:
The entire system... *(Consulting a file.)* No, there's no box for that. I'm listening…

JOAN:
First of all: nobody likes washing their hair that much. NOBODY. Second of all, a shampoo ad is not a shampoo ad. It's part of an industry that spends billions and billions of dollars for the sole purpose of making me feel ugly. Making me feel so ugly and disgusting and uncomfortable in my own skin that I'll believe I have to buy something to be beautiful. The ad industry is about hypnosis; it's about mass brainwashing; it's about social control. Third: when I graffiti an ad, it's not vandalism. It's resistance. It's my way of learning to love my thighs, my zits, my oily hair. So for me, vandalizing a shampoo ad is my way of standing up and saying to the whole universe: SCREW YOU, I'M ALREADY BEAUTIFUL!

Pause.

THE PRINCIPAL:
Give me a moment. *(Entering a number.)* Hello, Sandra. It's me. You're right: I do sleep with my

mouth open and I do look like Quasimodo. But that's no excuse for dumping me by text message. SCREW YOU, I'M ALREADY BEAUTIFUL!

He hangs up; pulls himself together; and scribbles on a piece of paper which he hands to JOAN.

JOAN:
What's this?

THE PRINCIPAL:
Your punishment. I'm ordering you to run for student council. This school needs girls like you. Don't you want to leave your mark on something more than ads? *(Beat.)* It's either that, or a whole week of detention.

JOAN:
You can't do that!

THE PRINCIPAL:
Sure, I can: it's called power. If you want some, you know what to do.

JOAN:
Me? Student Council President? It'd be like selling my soul to a corporation… On the other hand… Maybe you need to be part of the system to destroy it? I'm in the hallway when a girl comes out of the bathroom, sobbing. She says to me: "The Ad is right: my face is a mistake." I roll up my sleeves, take a deep breath, and walk into the bathroom.

THE SHAMPOO AD:
Joan! Wanna buy some –

JOAN:
I'm not Joan. I'm your future president. My number one mission: kicking you out of this school. SCREW YOU, your days are numbered and mine are just beginning. JOAN CRUST FOR PRESIDENT!

Scene 2: The Encyclopedia of Useless Facts

OLIVIER:
I'm looking at the most beautiful gift I've ever seen in my life. The wrapping is so perfect, I'm almost afraid to tear it.

> THE VOICE OF THE MAN IN A SUIT AND TIE:
> Go on. Open it…

OLIVIER:
Who is that? That's not my dad's voice.

> THE VOICE OF THE MAN IN A SUIT AND TIE:
> Tear...

OLIVIER:
Or my mom's. I look up.

> THE VOICE OF THE MAN IN A SUIT AND TIE:
> Destroy…

OLIVIER:
There's a man in a suit and tie. He's weird, but I can't exactly say why…

> THE VOICE OF THE MAN IN A SUIT AND TIE:
> Beauty never lasts.

OLIVIER:
I start unwrapping the present. I untie the ribbon. I slowly tear the paper, trying not to crumple it.

> THE VOICE OF A WITHERED OLD WOMAN:
> Hurry.

OLIVIER:
I look up. Standing beside the man in a suit and tie, there's a withered old woman. Clutching a baby.

THE VOICE OF A WITHERED OLD WOMAN:
Please. Hurry.

OLIVIER:
Who are these people? Why are they in my living room? I turn back to my present and finish unwrapping it.

THE VOICE OF THE MAN IN A SUIT AND TIE:
Beauty never lasts.

THE VOICE OF A WITHERED OLD WOMAN:
Hurry.

OLIVIER:
I take the lid off; I look inside the box… It's… It's Planet Earth. I take it out of the box and hold it in my hands. As I look closer, I start seeing… holes and stains.

THE VOICE OF THE ONE WHO IS THIRSTY:
I'm thirsty…

OLIVIER:
Storms and smoke.

THE VOICE OF THE ONE WHO IS HUNGRY:
I'm hungry…

OLIVIER:
It's like the Earth is turning into a… a tumour.

THE VOICE OF THE ONE WHO IS HOT:
I'm hot…

THE VOICE OF THE ONE WHO IS HURTING:
I hurt…

OLIVIER:
I see children toiling, nations bleeding…

THE VOICE OF THE MAN IN A SUIT AND TIE:
Beauty cannot last.

OLIVIER:
I see families fleeing and wailing, others sinking to the bottom of the ocean...

THE VOICE OF A WITHERED OLD WOMAN:
Hurry.

OLIVIER:
I see... I see babies... babies on a spit... roasting over a campfire…

THE VOICE OF THE MAN IN A SUIT AND TIE:
Marshmallows!

THE VOICE OF THE ONE WHO IS HUNGRY:
I'm hungry…

OLIVIER:
I look up. The woman and her baby are melting.

THE VOICE OF THE MAN IN A SUIT AND TIE:
Marshmallows!

OLIVIER:
They open their mouths, but it's not cries that come out: it's flies.

THE VOICE OF THE MAN IN A SUIT AND TIE:
Marshmallows!

OLIVIER:
And suddenly, I see what's wrong with the man in a suit and tie: he has gold teeth, and holes where his eyes should be.

ALL OF THE VOICES:
(To the tune of "Happy Birthday".) Happy Doomsday to you,

OLIVIER:
No...

ALL OF THE VOICES:
Happy Doomsday to you,

OLIVIER:
No...

ALL OF THE VOICES:
Happy Doomsday, dear Olivier, happy Doomsday to you.

OLIVIER:
No!

He wakes up with a start.

OLIVIER'S MOM:
Pancakes or omelette?

OLIVIER:
Did you know a lot of people won't have any breakfast today?!

OLIVIER'S MOM:
Exactly. So, eat for them.

OLIVIER:
I just dreamed I got our dying Earth as a gift.

OLIVIER'S MOM:
A dream?! What do you think it means?

OLIVIER:
The message seems pretty clear to me...

OLIVIER'S MOM:
Let me get my dream dictionary. Here we go... Getting a cat... getting a filling... getting a gift... getting Earth as a gift... getting our dying Earth as a gift... *(She reads, and quickly stops.)* Oh... That's not good.

OLIVIER:
Yeah, no kidding… What does it say?

OLIVIER'S MOM:
It says: "You're screwed. We're screwed. All of humanity is screwed." Never mind, it's just a book... Hey, what if you stopped watching documentaries? I've seen your search history. I know what you're googling: *Global warming. Overpopulation. Images of migrant families drowning in the ocean.* Why can't you act like a normal fourteen-year-old and watch anime and porn? I think you'd have better dreams...

OLIVIER:
I'm fifteen. Not fourteen.

OLIVIER'S MOM:
My God, it goes by fast.

OLIVIER:
Exactly. We don't have much time left to save the Earth.

OLIVIER'S MOM:
Save the Earth, save the Earth... I've still got three loads of laundry to do. Here's twenty bucks. Go buy a comic book.

OLIVIER:
Money isn't the solution, IT'S THE PROBLEM.

OLIVIER'S MOM:
Money's the problem? Good one! How exactly do you think we pay for your Internet?!

OLIVIER:
So, I decide to take the money – and some pancakes – and go straight to a bookstore. But not for a comic book.

OLIVIER:
Hello. I'm looking for a book about the environmental ravages of capitalism and the neoliberal system. It's called *Life Is a Fatal Illness; Humanity, a Cancer; Money, a Scourge; Death, Death Is Everywhere.*

THE WOMAN WHO SELLS BOOKS WHILE DRUNK:
Bleagh. How about a martini instead?

OLIVIER:
No. I'd rather have the book.

THE WOMAN WHO SELLS BOOKS WHILE DRUNK:
Geez... So serious so young.

She serves him a martini. With difficulty.

OLIVIER:
Are you drunk?

THE WOMAN WHO SELLS BOOKS WHILE DRUNK:
Pfffft... I haven't had a drink for two days. Except for yesterday. And this morning.

OLIVIER:
You're obviously drunk. It's sad to see you like this.

THE WOMAN WHO SELLS BOOKS WHILE DRUNK:
Know what I find sad? A fourteen-year-old kid buying a book with a title that'd make ya put a bullet in your head.

OLIVIER:
I'm fifteen. Not fourteen.

THE WOMAN WHO SELLS BOOKS WHILE DRUNK:
Even worse. You should be out there kissing and drinking and smoking and shoplifting. You're a downer. One look at you and I'm exhausted.

OLIVIER:
Sorry. I'm trying to save the Earth.

THE WOMAN WHO SELLS BOOKS WHILE DRUNK:
Saving the Earth is great. Keep it up! But don't forget to see that it's beautiful. Here. Read this. It'll help.

OLIVIER:
(Reading the title.) The Encyclopedia of Useless Facts.

THE WOMAN WHO SELLS BOOKS WHILE DRUNK:
Did you know that a cockroach can live seven days with no head? SEVEN DAYS. NO HEAD.

OLIVIER:
Wow…

THE WOMAN WHO SELLS BOOKS WHILE DRUNK:
Imagine what else is possible if a cockroach can live seven days with no head. SEVEN DAYS. NO HEAD.

OLIVIER:
Okay, I'll take it. How much?

THE WOMAN WHO SELLS BOOKS WHILE DRUNK:
You don't buy books like this. You steal them.

OLIVIER:
I'd never do that. I'm not a criminal.

THE WOMAN WHO SELLS BOOKS WHILE DRUNK:
(Beguilingly.) Did you know that we're about eight millimetres taller in the morning than in the evening? Or that our hair grows twice as fast on an airplane? Or that koalas are the only animals with fingerprints almost identical to those of humans? Not monkeys. Not bears. KOALAS!

OLIVIER:
(Running out without paying.) DON'T TELL MY MOM!

THE WOMAN WHO SELLS BOOKS WHILE DRUNK:
See, that's what I call "taking a bite out of life"! *(Pouring herself a martini.)* And don't forget to save the Earth. Please. Save the Earth.

Tuesday – The Campaign

Scene 3: I'm Not a Ghost

JOAN:
Tuesday morning, I don't go to school. I go straight to City Hall. Since I don't have an appointment, they won't let me in. I say, "No problem" and walk out… As soon as no one's looking, I jump a fence, scale a wall, break a window, and go inside.

JOAN:
Hello, Madam Mayor. My name is Joan Crust and I'm here to ask your advice on politics.

THE MAYOR:
First piece of advice: people usually use the door. Second piece of advice: change your name. "Crust" will never sell.

JOAN:
Your secretary wouldn't let me in. I don't have much time, so I had to get... creative.

THE MAYOR:
Determination... Love it. What can I do for you?

JOAN:
I'm running for student council and –

THE MAYOR:
You'd like to read me your speech and get my feedback. I'm listening.

Beat.

JOAN:
(To an imaginary crowd.) Hello.

I'm as surprised as all of you that I'm running for student council president. At first, I just did it to get out of a detention that was TOTALLY UNFAIR. But then I realized: deciding not to get involved involves consequences. Saying nothing means saying "yes." And when I look around me, I cannot bring myself to say yes.

As far as the system's concerned, I'm nobody. I've got no money, no vote, no job. But somehow, here I am, in flesh and blood. I'm not a ghost. I want to be able to touch things. Move things. Change things. The world has an effect on me: I want to have an effect on the world.

For starters, I pledge to get ads out of our school. Even more importantly, I want us to get them out of our heads and replace them with one simple message: our actions are real. We exist.

These elections are my way of leaving something behind other than my carbon footprint. I don't want to just take from the Earth. I want to give back. Yes, I want to leave my mark: but it's not about ego. I don't want to go down in History: I want History to have a future.

The MAYOR sheds a tear.

JOAN:
Are you... are you crying?!

THE MAYOR:
Yeah. *(Showing her a smartphone.)* Look at this kitten. It's wearing mittens.

JOAN:
What about my speech?

THE MAYOR:
What speech? Oh yeah, your speech. How can I put this: no, no, no, no, no, no, and no. Two major problems: what you're saying and what you're

wearing. The solution is, empty promises. Tell them what they want to hear, then do what you want once you're elected. Now, about your appearance: remember that you're a woman going into politics. People will talk about your clothes, not your ideas. So, you might as well make sure they have nice things to say. Here, try this. *(Handing her a wig identical to the one worn by the SHAMPOO AD.)* Yes! Much better.

JOAN:
I feel fake.

THE MAYOR:
That's a great start. Now that we want to look at you, we might want to listen to you.

Beat.

JOAN:
Can I see the picture of the kitten? Aw: it is really cute.

THE MAYOR:
Look: it's wearing mittens…

JOAN:
Little mittens…

THE MAYOR:
Little mittens…

JOAN:
Little mittens... *(Hurling the telephone against the wall.)* Do you see mittens on my hands? No! You know why? Because I'm going to spend my career like I spend my life: with my claws out. I'm running in this election – no wig, no empty promises, with my real name – and I'm going to win. And once I've kicked ads out of this school, I'm going to kick you out of City Hall.

THE MAYOR:
You're not going to win, sweetie. And I'm going to buy myself a new phone with your parents' taxes.

JOAN:
(Running away.) THERE IS NO JUSTICE!

Scene 4: Spreading the Good News

OLIVIER:
The Encyclopedia of Useless Facts: I've read it and read it, learned it off by heart, recited it. I've made it my Bible. And when I have good news, I share it. I share it at the grocery store:

> OLIVIER:
> Did you know that a cockroach can live seven days with no head? SEVEN DAYS! NO HEAD!
>
> THE GROCERY STORE CASHIER:
> That'll be $9.58. Points card?

OLIVIER:
I share it with the woman who drives the bus…

> OLIVIER:
> Did you know that in the States, vending machines kill four times as many people a year as sharks!
>
> THE WOMAN WHO DRIVES THE BUS:
> Here's $20. Go take a cab.

OLIVIER:
I don't want money: I want a reaction. Maybe I need a different strategy... When I get to school, I decide to change my approach.

> OLIVIER:
> Hello! It's "Future Week." What do you want to be when you grow up?
>
> GABRIELLA:
> I'm gonna be an influencer.

OLIVIER:
Great! What do you want to talk about?

GABRIELLA:
I don't need to talk. Have you seen my boobs?!

OLIVIER:
Wow. They are very nice. Did you know that babies are born with 300 bones, while adults only have 206?

GABRIELLA:
I don't need bones: I've got boobs.

The next person:

OLIVIER:
Hello! It's "Future Week." What do you want to be when you grow up?

NORT:
Thanatologist.

OLIVIER:
What's that?

NORT:
Embalmer. Ever since I was a kid. I stare at people and imagine I'm draining their blood.

OLIVIER:
Uh... Did you know that our fingernails grow four times as fast as our toenails?

NORT:
You have pale skin. You'll make a good corpse.

OLIVIER:
Am I safe here?

NORT:
No one is safe.

The next person:

OLIVIER:
Hello! It's "Future Week." What do you want to be when you grow up?

JOEY:
When I will grow up, I was a teacher.

OLIVIER:
That makes no sense.

JOEY:
Sorry. When I *shall* grow up, I was a teacher.

OLIVIER:
Did you know that –

JOEY:
Whoa. I hate learning.

OLIVIER:
Oh, come on. Why can't I manage to spread the good news? I guess I should talk to someone who really needs help. Someone whose life is difficult, dark, depressing.

OLIVIER:
Hey there, Principal!

THE PRINCIPAL:
Who are you?

OLIVIER:
Good question, my friend! If you'd asked me a few days ago, I would have said: "Sir, I'm a guy who wants to go hide in a bunker before the next nuclear war breaks out." But now, my answer would be: "Hi! I'm Olivier and I want to write *The Encyclopedia of Useless Facts, Volume 2!*" There are so many extraordinary things we don't know. For example: do you know how many teeth a snail has?

THE PRINCIPAL:
I don't feel like –

OLIVIER:
Pick a number! Pick a number!

THE PRINCIPAL:
One.

OLIVIER:
No. More!

THE PRINCIPAL:
Two.

OLIVIER:
No. More!

THE PRINCIPAL:
Three.

OLIVIER:
No. More!

THE PRINCIPAL:
Four.

OLIVIER:
No. More!

THE PRINCIPAL:
Five.

OLIVIER:
No. More!

THE PRINCIPAL:
If it's thirty, this is gonna get tedious.

OLIVIER:
14,000! Snails have an average of 14,000 teeth. Fascinating, right?!

THE PRINCIPAL:
I haven't got time to be fascinated…

OLIVIER:
That's your problem right there! That's why you're unhappy.

THE PRINCIPAL:
I'm not unhappy. I am indifferent to life in general and human beings in particular.

OLIVIER:
HEY! You're a downer. One look at you and I'm exhausted. Optimism is a muscle. You have to use it or else it withers. So try, before it's too late.

Beat.

THE PRINCIPAL:
You know what I did yesterday? I wiped my mother's ass. I went to visit her at the home she lives in and there was poop everywhere. It was like she'd said to herself: "Hey, I'm gonna take a dump AND run around at the same time." I got some toilet paper; I laid my mother over my knees; and I wiped her. I wiped her once, twice, too many times. I wiped my mother until she was clean. Like she did for me when I was a baby.

Beat.

OLIVIER:
Don't you pay people in there to do that?

THE PRINCIPAL:
Sure. I pay them a lot. But I've got news for you: there are way more people who poop than people who wipe. Is that written in your book?

OLIVIER goes to leave, then changes his mind.

OLIVIER:
Did you know that sea lions hold each other's hands while they sleep? That way, even if the ocean currents carry them away in the night, they never wake up alone. That means that, thanks to you, your mother will never be alone, lost at sea. You're a good son. Even if your mother can't speak anymore, or thank you, or recognize you, you're a good son.

Beat.

THE PRINCIPAL:
I know you can't see it in my face, but thank you. You're able to be touched by someone else's life, Olivier. That's very precious. I don't have it. Sandra certainly doesn't have it –

OLIVIER:
Who's Sandra?

THE PRINCIPAL:
IT DOESN'T MATTER... But you have it: the gift of empathy. *(Beat.)* You are running for president.

OLIVIER:
Is that a question?

THE PRINCIPAL:
No. The speeches are tomorrow.

OLIVIER:
Me? A speech? No way. I hate public speaking. The more people are watching me, the more tongue-tied I get.

THE PRINCIPAL:
Olivier, until now, I thought getting old was a punishment, life kicking the crap out of us with its dirty rotten invisible boots. After talking to you, I think getting old is a punishment, life kicking the crap out of us with its dirty rotten invisible boots.

OLIVIER:
Isn't that the same thing?

THE PRINCIPAL:
Yes, but that's not the point. The point is that you're not old. You're full of energy and hope and innocence and optimism. And that's contagious.

OLIVIER:
But... But I have no campaign platform. I don't see what I can –

OLIVIER looks at The Encyclopedia of Useless Facts. *A moment of revelation.*

OLIVIER:
The principal is right: this is my chance to do for other people what this book does for me. I go home, go to my room, and picture the entire school looking at me. I throw up. Then I start writing my speech.

Scene 5: Rescue Dolls

JOAN:
That evening, I'm still steamed from my visit to the Mayor. Good timing, because I have my weekly visit to the shrink.

THE PSYCHOLOGIST:
How's your anger management going?

JOAN:
I don't need anger management. Why would you say that? WANT ME TO BREAK YOUR FACE?

THE PSYCHOLOGIST:
Why do you think you're mad all the time, Joan?

JOAN:
I'm not mad: it's just that people are so maddening.

THE PSYCHOLOGIST:
And what makes people so maddening?

JOAN:
What makes people so maddening? Come on: how long has it been since you OPENED YOUR EYES?

THE PSYCHOLOGIST:
Don't you ever get tired of yelling?

JOAN:
YES! BUT I DON'T KNOW WHAT ELSE TO DO!

THE PSYCHOLOGIST:
You can start by dropping your guard and opening up. You know, Joan, a shield is useful. But it's heavy. Tell me about what you do to feel better.

JOAN:
(After a beat.) You signed a confidentiality clause, right?

THE PSYCHOLOGIST:
What you say stays between you and me.

JOAN:
And if it ever gets out, I can take you to court, get you fired, and make sure you're miserable for the rest of your life?

THE PSYCHOLOGIST:
That would be a bit extreme, but yes.

Beat.

JOAN:
Sometimes I go to my room, lock the door, and play with my dolls. Like when I was four years old. I pretend a Barbie is just a Barbie. Not a sexist toy dreamed up by the patriarchy to give me a future eating disorder. Just a Barbie. I dress her. I pick out her shoes. And I pour her tea. For a while, I take a vacation from the end of the world. That's my cure for the future: going back to a past where I didn't know enough to worry.

THE PSYCHOLOGIST:
So, when becoming an adult frightens you, you choose to go back to being a child? *(JOAN nods.)* Have you found other ways to reduce your anxiety?

JOAN:
Yeah. Running for student council. Believing I can change the world makes me want to be a part of it.

A timer goes off, indicating the end of the session.

THE PSYCHOLOGIST:
You would make an excellent president, Joan.

JOAN:
Thanks. *(Beat.)* I think so, too.

Wednesday – The Debate

Scene 6: Speeches in Front of the Entire School

THE PRINCIPAL:
Hello. Welcome to –

SOMEONE IN THE CROWD:
Shut up.

THE PRINCIPAL:
YOU SHUT UP. At least I get paid to be here. Welcome to Day 3 of our thrilling Future Week. *(Sound of a cheesy party horn.)* Today we are pleased to introduce the blah blah blah... Let's get this over with. First candidate. Joan.

JOAN:
(Beginning to read her speech.) Hello. I –

THE PRINCIPAL:
One minute per speech. After that, I cut the mic and throw it in the garbage.

JOAN:
ONE MINUTE?! I can't possibly mobilize the masses in –

THE PRINCIPAL:
45 seconds.

JOAN crumples up her speech.

JOAN:
Dear students – male, female, and other magnificent creatures: genderfluid, postbinary and/or gender nonconforming – hello. My name is Joan Crust and here's my basic platform: screw school, screw classes, screw ads, screw it all. Let's start over.

THE ENTIRE SCHOOL:
Screw it all! Screw it all! Screw it all!

JOAN:
Sure, it'll take some effort, but…

SOMEONE IN THE CROWD:
Effort? Ugh.

The crowd boos.

THE PRINCIPAL:
Speaking of making an effort, here's your second candidate: Olivier.

OLIVIER looks at the crowd and freezes, hyperventilating.

THE PRINCIPAL:
45 seconds.

OLIVIER:
I...

THE PRINCIPAL:
30 seconds.

OLIVIER:
I... The...

THE PRINCIPAL:
15 seconds.

OLIVIER:
Did you know… I... Microorganisms… Hurray for optimism.

JOAN:
Hurray for optimism? BS! Optimism is part of the problem. We can't sleepwalk through this! We have to speak the truth: Fire! Fire! Our house is on fire, and if we do nothing, we'll burn right along with it!

OLIVIER:
I... The...

THE PRINCIPAL:
Here he goes again…

OLIVIER:
I... Life is great.

THE PRINCIPAL:
And because life is not only great, but also long, here is our final candidate.

JOAN:
Another candidate? What do you mean, another candidate?! I thought it was just the two of us!

THE PRINCIPAL:
Everyone: this is Mike.

MIKE:
(Slow, dopey, tentative.) Hey. *(Silence.)* I'm Mike. *(Silence.)* If I win, my folks'll buy pizza for everybody. *(Thunderous applause.)* Extra bacon.

The crowd goes wild.

THE ENTIRE SCHOOL:
Mike! Mike! Mike! Mike! Mike!

THE PRINCIPAL:
Don't forget: you have all afternoon to vote, but you don't have to. The less you vote, the faster we count. We'll announce the results tomorrow. Bye.

JOAN and OLIVIER are left alone.

JOAN:
You do realize that a pizza is going to win this election? *(OLIVIER nods: beat.)* What were you going to say about microorganisms in your speech, anyway? I didn't really get it...

OLIVIER:
I wanted to say: "Hello, entire school. Thank you for coming. Did you know that there are more microorganisms living on our skin than humans inhabiting the Earth. Each of us is a zoo. A planet. That means that, even when we're alone, we're not alone… If I'm elected president, I promise to share more fascinating trivia like that, every day. We'll call it "Mellow Middays." It'll help us build up the muscle of our optimism. And optimism is essential. Also – good news! – it's contagious. *(Beat.)* You're right: there's a fire. Our house is on fire. But if we forget that the house is beautiful, we won't fight to save it.

Beat.

JOAN:
Have you ever dreamed of getting our dying Earth as a gift?

OLIVIER:
At least once a week. But I'm not sure it's just a dream.

OLIVIER AND JOAN:
(To the tune of "Happy Birthday".) Happy Doomsday to us...

Beat.

JOAN:
I changed the globe in my bedroom: I replaced my Blue Planet with a Barren Planet. I need people to see what I see in my dreams. It's like my graffiti. You understand some things better with your eyes than with your head.

Beat.

OLIVIER:
Here.

JOAN:
What's this?

OLIVIER:
It's *The Encyclopedia of Useless Facts.* It helps me. Turn to any page and – look out! – it could change your life.

JOAN:
(Opening the book.) "Did you know that two-year-olds can suffer from depression?"

OLIVIER:
Oops… Not that page. Try another one.

JOAN turns to another page and starts to read in silence. She seems to be more and more fascinated.

OLIVIER:
What is it? What is it?

JOAN:
Did you know that the total weight of ants on Earth is greater than that of humans?!

OLIVIER:
Yep. Sure, they're small and easy to squish, but there's so many of them that when you put them all together *(As it begins to dawn on him.)* they weigh more than you'd ev –

JOAN:
SCREW THE ELECTION! The two of us weigh more than a pizza! I have a plan.

OLIVIER:
She explains her plan. It's an excellent plan, so I tell her –

OLIVIER:
I can't do that! One: it's against the law. Two: what if we get caught?

JOAN:
I don't know. But we know what happens if we do nothing…

OLIVIER:
If I say no, will you go do it by yourself?

JOAN:
No. I'll do it with my microorganisms, but it won't be as much fun. At least tonight, they and I won't dream the Earth is dying. We'll dream we tried to hold its hand.

OLIVIER:
I know you're just saying that to manipulate me.

JOAN:
Is it working?

Beat.

OLIVIER:
Yeah, it's working.

Scene 7: Ninja Style

OLIVIER and JOAN dress up as ninjas.

OLIVIER:
We wait until the afternoon is over and everyone has voted, then we hide in our lockers.

JOAN:
Four p.m. to nine p.m.: I eat little pieces of cheese and wait for the extracurricular nerds to leave the building.

OLIVIER:
I don't eat anything. There's nothing in my locker.

JOAN:
Nine p.m. to midnight: I eat little pieces of carrot and wait for the janitors to leave the building.

OLIVIER:
I don't eat anything. There's nothing in my locker.

JOAN:
Midnight. I come out and stretch: eight hours in a locker is a long time.

OLIVIER:
I don't come out. I'm having a hypoglycemic episode…

JOAN:
I get him out of his locker. I slap him a few times and give him some nuts and juice. 12:15. We go down Hallway D…

OLIVIER:
Hallway C, Hallway B...

JOAN:
And we run into a janitor... DAMMIT.

> THE JANITOR:
> Hello. Are you lost?
>
> JOAN:
> Uh... Nous pas parler le English.
>
> THE JANITOR
> Êtes-vous perdus?
>
> OLIVIER:
> Uh... No hablamos French-o.
>
> THE JANITOR:
> ¿Están perdidos?
>
> JOAN:
> Can you stop being so bilingual!!
>
> THE JANITOR:
> Nein. Auf Wiedersehen!

JOAN:
He points us toward the exit. We thank him... and run the other way. We take a different route.

OLIVIER:
Hallway C…

JOAN:
Hallway D…

OLIVIER:
Hallway E…

JOAN:
Second floor, Hallway F, G…

OLIVIER:
(Out of breath.) We catch our breath…

JOAN:
YOU catch your breath... Go?

OLIVIER:
Not yet…

JOAN:
Now?

OLIVIER:
Gimme a sec…

JOAN:
How about now?

OLIVIER:
Almost…

JOAN:
Go?

OLIVIER:
Go!

OLIVIER:
Hallway H, I, main floor, Hallway A... And finally, we get to the Admin Office.

JOAN:
I try to open the door with a debit card, a screwdriver, a bobby pin…

OLIVIER:
Whereas I simply turn the doorknob, because the door is unlocked…

THE PRINCIPAL:
Good evening. What are you doing here?

OLIVIER:
She did it! Joan Crust! It was her idea! Don't tell my mom! Please!

JOAN:
ARGH! We're just… lost.

THE PRINCIPAL:
No, I don't think so...

JOAN:
We came to protest.

OLIVIER:
I didn't come to protest. Sorry!

JOAN:
SCREW ADS!

THE PRINCIPAL:
It's one a.m. Keep it down. Do you like playing volleyball, Joan?

JOAN:
Don't try to change the subject. It won't work. SCREW ADS!

THE PRINCIPAL:
Do you like playing volleyball? You must like it: I see you playing almost every lunch hour.

JOAN:
I love it. I imagine that the other team is the corporations dominating the agri-food sector... and I spike them in the face, the face, ALWAYS THE FACE.

THE PRINCIPAL:
Five years ago, gym class was in the cafeteria. Back then, when it stank, you never knew if it was the soup or the kids. You don't want that… We had to find a solution. The renovations – by which I mean the new gym – came as soon as we got the ad revenues. *(Beat.)* Might you not, in fact, actually be here to illegally modify the election results?

JOAN:
No. Why would you think that?

THE PRINCIPAL:
You're holding a pile of fake ballots. And you're dressed as ninjas.

OLIVIER:
Guilty! We're guilty! We did it!

THE PRINCIPAL:
Also, the night janitor told me that a girl and boy who speak neither English, nor French, nor Spanish, nor German were running around the school "looking for the exit." Besides, there are cameras. Everywhere. It must have been pretty boring inside your lockers, right?

OLIVIER:
So boring… It was dark. I was hot then cold. Hungry then thirsty.

JOAN:
We have no choice. We can't let Mike win.

THE PRINCIPAL:
There are two of you. Who are you voting for?

OLIVIER:
Joan! I never want to speak in public again. Ever.

THE PRINCIPAL:
So, to sum up your offences: lying, breaking and entering, and corruption.

JOAN:
You want real elections? You got 'em. THERE IS NO JUSTICE!

THE PRINCIPAL:
Speaking of justice: do you not find it ironic that you are ready to subvert a democratic process in order to impose your personal beliefs? Isn't that a – what's that word again – dictatorship?

JOAN doesn't have an answer, so she breaks something.

THE PRINCIPAL:
Lying, breaking and entering, corruption, AND property damage.

OLIVIER:
Why'd you do that?

JOAN:
Because I can see his point, and I've got nothing.

THE PRINCIPAL:
It's up to you to choose which world you want to live in. Is it one where you do exactly what you claim to despise, or one in which you truly give democracy a chance? *(Beat.)* You know, I've been working here for twenty years now. I'll tell you something: kids – and adults – are always at their dumbest when they're in a group. Unfortunately, IQs don't add up: they divide each other. I'm convinced that once the students were alone with their ballots, they made a rational and enlightened choice. You've got to learn to have faith. People are not as stupid as we think.

Pause. JOAN and OLIVIER glance at each other and, not without misgivings, tear up their fake ballots.

OLIVIER:
Why do you never show this side of yourself when you're talking to the entire school?

THE PRINCIPAL:
Precisely because I, too, find it easier to be intelligent when I'm not in a group. Besides, I save what's left of my energy for my mother.

JOAN:
What's wrong with your mother?

THE PRINCIPAL:
She's lost everything, that's all. Everything but my vote.

Thursday – The Results

Scene 8: D-E-A-D

OLIVIER:
On the morning of the elections, I decide to stop at the bookstore to thank… I don't even know her name, but she changed my life.

OLIVIER:
Excuse me. I'm looking for the woman who sells books while drunk.

THE BOOKSTORE OWNER:
She doesn't work here anymore because, as you say, she sells books while drunk.

OLIVIER:
Do you know where I can find her?

THE BOOKSTORE OWNER:
At home or in a bar. Oh, no, wait: she's dead.

OLIVIER:
(Gobsmacked.) What?

THE BOOKSTORE OWNER:
Dead. DEH-duh. D-e-a-d. She's DEAD.

OLIVIER:
But... no.

THE BOOKSTORE OWNER:
But... yes.

OLIVIER:
You just said that you fired her.

THE BOOKSTORE OWNER:
That's right. And then, she died.

OLIVIER:
How?

THE BOOKSTORE OWNER:
Her. A bus. *(He mimes the bus running over her.)* Pudding.

OLIVIER:
I mean... How can you tell me that like that…

THE BOOKSTORE OWNER:
Sorry. *(Singing.) Her, a bus, pudding!* "Blind spot"? They oughtta call it a "dead spot."

OLIVIER:
It kinda... seems like you don't care.

THE BOOKSTORE OWNER:
You're right. I haven't had an emotion since 1999.

OLIVIER:
I had so much to tell her… What was her name?

THE BOOKSTORE OWNER:
I don't know. She was an employee. Why would I know her name?

OLIVIER:
You're a monster.

THE BOOKSTORE OWNER:
Good. In business, that's an advantage.

OLIVIER:
I walk out of the bookstore. I feel the muscle of my optimism wither. Then disappear. I go to school.

THE PRINCIPAL:
Hello. Welcome to –

SOMEONE IN THE CROWD:
Shut up.

THE PRINCIPAL:
YOU SHUT UP. At least *my* dad's not in jail. Welcome to the announcement of our student council president. Before we proceed, I would like to thank our amazing blah blah blah… So, it is with, um, an emotion, that I give you your new president... *(opening an envelope)* Mike.

THE ENTIRE SCHOOL:
Pizza! Pizza! Pizza!

THE PRINCIPAL:
(Looking at JOAN and OLIVIER.) Sorry.

MIKE:
Hey. *(Beat.)* Thanks. *(Beat.)* Enjoy your pizza.

THE ENTIRE SCHOOL:
Pizza! Pizza! Pizza!

JOAN, enraged, leaps in front of the mic.

JOAN:
(Struggling not to fall apart.) CRAP MEDALS! That's what we deserve… Not pizza, not democracy, not a future. Just medals made of... of... of...

She runs away, unable to hold back her tears. OLIVIER helplessly watches her go.

OLIVIER:
I want to follow Joan, but I can't move. I want to scream at the students to stop laughing, but I can't speak. That's my life, right there: wanting things and not being able to do them. I go home.

OLIVIER'S MOM:
How come you're not at school?

OLIVIER:
Mom, what do you do to be happy?

OLIVIER'S MOM:
What do I do to be happy? What a question… Want a sandwich?

OLIVIER:
THIS IS AN EMERGENCY.

OLIVIER'S MOM:
Okay, gimme a sec… Oh! Got it. Go on. Try me again.

OLIVIER:
Mom, what do you do to be happy?

OLIVIER'S MOM:
I only ask myself questions I know the answers to. Like: how many more loads of laundry? One. I know the answer: I'm happy. Why do I do laundry? To have clean clothes that smell nice. Nailed it: I feel good! What is the meaning of life and the universe? Uh-oh... I have a headache.

OLIVIER:
So, it's better not to think?

OLIVIER'S MOM:
Now he gets it! The less you know, the better you feel.

OLIVIER:
It's like I can't help wondering about the meaning of things.

OLIVIER'S MOM:
The meaning of things… The meaning of things… Don't turn left, don't turn right, go straight ahead on the highway of life.

OLIVIER:
But what if that highway leads directly into a wall?

OLIVIER'S MOM:
Uh... I... I never thought of that. That would be sad, huh? That would mean… We'd have to... We'd have to change the way... the way we live. *(Beat: thinking.)* ARGH! What've you done to me? My brain is melting! You're contagious, now.

OLIVIER:
Suddenly I see it in her eyes. My mother has a profound desire to help me, but my questions are too big for her. And like all adults who want to help someone but don't know how, she ends up saying:

OLIVIER'S MOM:
Get your shoes on. I'm taking you to a therapist.

THE THERAPIST:
So, Olivier. Why are you here?

OLIVIER'S MOM:
He thinks too much. He asks questions with no answers. He's always –

THE THERAPIST:
Ma'am, I need to ask you to go back to the waiting room. It's your son I want to talk to. *(She leaves.)* So, Olivier: what's on your mind?

OLIVIER:
I think about my nightmares; my documentaries; everyone who voted for Mike; and I say: "The future scares me."

THE THERAPIST:
Olivier… I regret to inform you that you are lucid.

OLIVIER:
Is there a cure?

THE THERAPIST:
It won't be easy, but yes. Is that what you want?

OLIVIER:
Yes.

THE THERAPIST:
You sure?

OLIVIER:
Yeah. I'm exhausted. What do you suggest?

THE THERAPIST:
(Handing him a pair of glasses.) This. Four times a day. Ready? *(OLIVIER nods and puts on the glasses.)* Three, two, one…

Lights. Music. Screens. Whirlwind.

– *"Baby! Baby! Dance floor!"*
– Hello! Welcome to a show where people judge each other, eliminate each other, and wear bikinis.

A WOMAN applies shampoo and approaches orgasm.

– *"Baby! Baby! Dance floor!"*
– Hello! Welcome to a show where people sing, eliminate each other, and try to make you cry.
– Then I lost my mom and the use of both my legs.
– Super! Now let's hear you sing Leonard Cohen's "Hallelujah."

A WOMAN chews gum and approaches orgasm.

– *"Baby! Baby! Dance floor!"*
– And that's when I found out I'd inherited Dad's leukemia.
– Super! Now let's hear your duet: Celine Dion's "I'm Alive."

A WOMAN applies lipstick and approaches orgasm.

- *"Baby! Baby! Dance floor!"*
- Live now. Pay nothing for a year.
- Live now. Pay nothing for two years.
- Live now. Pay for the rest of your life.
- *"Baby! Baby! Dance floor!"*
- *"Baby! Baby! Dance floor!"*
- *"BABY! BABY! DANCE FLOOR!"*

THE THERAPIST removes the glasses from OLIVIER.

THE THERAPIST:
How are you feeling, Olivier?

OLIVIER:
Baby... Baby... Dance floor...

THE THERAPIST:
Ma'am, your son is cured.

OLIVIER'S MOM:
Are you sure? Olivier, what do you think about offshore tax havens? *(No reaction.)* The Amazon rainforest? *(No reaction.)* The oil sands? *(OLIVIER hums the tune of "Hallelujah.")* He's cured! My son is cured!

THE THERAPIST and OLIVIER'S MOTHER come and join OLIVIER. They all hum "Hallelujah" in harmony.

Scene 9: Threat, Please

JOAN:
By the time I snap out of it, I'm home, in front of the Barren Planet. With a Barbie in my hands... all chewed up and scarred and missing a head. I tell myself: "You'll never be four years old again. Deal with it." Yeah, that was my first mistake: I thought I could smash the system AND play by the rules. But I was right all along: real power doesn't come from politics. It comes from action. We're motivated by fear. That's just the way humans are: it takes a threat for us to feel involved. Lucky for me, Friday's theme party involves everybody. Tomorrow, at school, I'm gonna leave my mark. I'm gonna leave it all over.

Friday – The Festivities

Scene 10: Two Wings of the Same F***ing Unicorn

OLIVIER:
I'm standing in front of a mirror. I try to smile, but I can't. I lift the corners of my mouth with my fingers, but it doesn't help. Suddenly, I hear pow. It sounds like a firecracker. Or a gunshot. I think "It's war," without knowing whether it's the one inside of me or outside of me. Another pow, even louder. Pow. Pow. It doesn't stop. I ask out loud: "What's going on?" Except that it doesn't sound like "What's going on," it sounds like "Wah oh-ih aw?" Then I get it. The pow is not a firecracker. Or a gun. It's my teeth exploding.

Multiple "pows" of exploding teeth. OLIVIER covers his mouth and runs around in a panic. THE WOMAN WHO SELLS BOOKS WHILE DRUNK appears.

THE WOMAN WHO SELLS BOOKS WHILE DRUNK:
Hey!

OLIVIER:
Ah! You ah ah-aye?! I ah sho hah-ee oo shee you!

THE WOMAN WHO SELLS BOOKS WHILE DRUNK:
I don't understand. Where are your teeth?

OLIVIER:
Ah oh-er.

THE WOMAN WHO SELLS BOOKS WHILE DRUNK:
Oh boy... You leave them alone for two seconds and they end up with no teeth. How are you gonna take a bite out of life with no teeth?!

She claps her hands. OLIVIER gets his teeth back.

OLIVIER:
I'm so happy to see you! Your boss told me you were dead.

THE WOMAN WHO SELLS BOOKS WHILE DRUNK:
I am. *(Showing him her abdomen.)* See? You can still see the tread-marks.

OLIVIER:
But you look great…

THE WOMAN WHO SELLS BOOKS WHILE DRUNK:
I know. They redid my face. A bus on your nose is not a good look.

OLIVIER:
I'm dreaming, right? That's what's happening?

THE WOMAN WHO SELLS BOOKS WHILE DRUNK:
Ah, don't sweat the details. Dreaming or not, I'm here: make the most of it! Let's talk about your therapy, and your new "glasses." Do you like them?

OLIVIER:
No, but they help. Since I stopped asking questions, I feel so light.

THE WOMAN WHO SELLS BOOKS WHILE DRUNK:
Light? Like a dead leaf? *(Silence.)* Olivier, I'm gonna show you something.

OLIVIER:
What?

THE WOMAN WHO SELLS BOOKS WHILE DRUNK:
My new home.

She claps her hands. They are suddenly transported somewhere else. Unicorns. Pan flute. An incessant shower of shooting stars.

THE WOMAN WHO SELLS BOOKS WHILE DRUNK:
Welcome to Paradise. Isn't it awful?

OLIVIER:
What's that?

THE WOMAN WHO SELLS BOOKS WHILE DRUNK:
A unicorn. They're like the squirrels of Paradise. Fu** off, I haven't got any food!

The swear words are censored by a beep.

OLIVIER:
What's that music?

THE WOMAN WHO SELLS BOOKS WHILE DRUNK:
Pan flute. More pan flute. Always and forever the f***ing pan flute.

OLIVIER:
Since when do you swear?

THE WOMAN WHO SELLS BOOKS WHILE DRUNK:
Since I'm not f***ing allowed to. *(She calls into the distance.)* Raoul, come here. *(RAOUL, an angel, appears, flying and playing a harp.)* Olivier, meet Raoul, THE ONE WHO TOLD EVERYBODY I HAD A FLASK SO THEY CONFISCATED IT... Raoul, meet Olivier.

RAOUL:
(Singing and strumming his harp... or not.) Olivier?! THE Olivier?!

OLIVIER:
You talk about me?

THE WOMAN WHO SELLS BOOKS WHILE DRUNK:
Sure. That's what happens when you die with no kid, no man, and no passion… Raoul, ask me if I'm going to the spa today.

RAOUL:
Why? We all know that a daily spa visit is mandatory.

OLIVIER:
You go to the spa every day? Wow.

THE WOMAN WHO SELLS BOOKS WHILE DRUNK:
Did you just say "wow"? What am I supposed to do with a Jacuzzi? "Is it too hot? Is it too cold?" HOW SHOULD I KNOW, I DON'T HAVE A BODY! Go on, Raoul: ask me if I want to go to the spa.

RAOUL:
I feel like this is a trap –

THE WOMAN WHO SELLS BOOKS WHILE DRUNK:
ASK ME.

RAOUL:
Oh sweet gentle friend, are you going to the spa today?

THE WOMAN WHO SELLS BOOKS WHILE DRUNK:
No. I refuse.

Sirens. Flashing lights. The unicorns run away. So does RAOUL.

THE CONTROL TOWER OF PARADISE:
Attention! Code 58. Repeat. Code 58.

OLIVIER:
What's going on?

THE WOMAN WHO SELLS BOOKS WHILE DRUNK:
It just so happens that I said the forbidden word.

OLIVIER:
Which one?

THE WOMAN WHO SELLS BOOKS WHILE DRUNK:
"No!"

THE CONTROL TOWER OF PARADISE:
Attention! Code 58, Repeat Offence. Code 58, Repeat Offence.

THE WOMAN WHO SELLS BOOKS WHILE DRUNK:
We're not allowed to say NO here! But saying NO is important! Saying NO lights up your heart! You need to know how to say no, no, no, no, no, no, NO!

THE CONTROL TOWER OF PARADISE:
Attention! All the codes! Repeat. All the codes. The crazy lady has f***ing lost it again!

Short circuit. The Control Tower of Paradise implodes. Everything is calm once more.

OLIVIER:
I tried. I'm not leadership material. Having influence is for influential people.

THE WOMAN WHO SELLS BOOKS WHILE DRUNK:
Olivier, changing the world is not just about protests. Or speaking to a crowd. It can be as simple as giving someone a book. Look at me: I died drunk, alone, and in debt. The way most people see it, not exactly a winner... Yet in spite of everything, I know I made a difference. I've seen it in your eyes. My contribution, my legacy, is you. You, and hundreds of books that will never be paid for. *(Beat.)* You live in a world where even a beating of wings can cause a tornado. Will you really choose to be a dead leaf?

OLIVIER:
I'll throw out my glasses. I'm sorry.

THE WOMAN WHO SELLS BOOKS WHILE DRUNK:
No. Keep them, but don't forget: entertainment is a nice break. Not a way of life. You have to stay angry. Then happy. Then angry. Then happy. They're just two wings of the same f***ing unicorn. Freedom, you g*dd*mn tight-a** motherf***ers! Freedom!

He wakes up with a start.

OLIVIER'S MOM:
Pancakes or omelette?

OLIVIER:
I DON'T WANT TO EAT. I WANT TO LIVE!

OLIVIER'S MOM:
Great: a relapse…

OLIVIER:
CAN YOU SEW?

OLIVIER'S MOM:
Sew? Why are you –

OLIVIER:
We have 15 minutes to make me a costume.

OLIVIER'S MOM:
I hope you know what costume you want, at least…

OLIVIER:
I know exactly what costume I want!

Scene 11: The Match

Cheesy party ambiance. THE PRINCIPAL is dressed as a sea lion.

THE PRINCIPAL:
Hello.

SOMEONE IN THE CROWD:
Shut up.

THE PRINCIPAL:
You shut up. At least *I'm* not dressed as a turd. Welcome to the final day of our thrilling Future Week. *(Sound of a cheesy party horn.... dying.)* As you know, I'm not one to make an effort. Or a speech. Or a compliment. However, I'd like to take this opportunity to thank our three candidates, especially those not named Mike. You, like me, work hard to take care of people who are incapable of appreciating it. It is for you that I am dressed as a sea lion. Thank you for holding out your hand to me and reminding me that... I don't remember what. Now, here is your president to announce the winner of the costume contest.

MIKE:
(Dressed as a boxer.) Uh...

Since his hands are encased in boxing gloves, MIKE can't manage to open the envelope. He tries... and tries... and tries... THE PRINCIPAL loses patience and snatches the envelope away. JOAN comes forward. She is dressed as a match. She is holding a gas can.

JOAN:
I win. How do I know? Because unlike the elections, this time I stuck to my plan. I didn't let luck – or other people – decide for me.

THE PRINCIPAL:
And the winner is... Joan Crust for her lovely "match" costume. A round of applause. A ROUND OF APPLAUSE. And that concludes my week. Bye.

He leaves. JOAN addresses the crowd.

JOAN:
I'm not dressed as a match. I'm dressed as an alarm clock. *(Beat.)* I've spent the past week saying that everything around us is on fire. I wish it had stayed a metaphor. *(JOAN pours gasoline on herself.)* That's right: don't help me. Don't run away. Take out your phones. I want everyone to hear what I have to say. *(She pours more gasoline.)* Violence is not just about hitting people. Violence is injustice. It's powerlessness. Violence is the rich deciding that the poor should stay poor. Violence is choosing to destroy the world because you have the luxury of not being part of it. Violence is having the power to decide for others without ever thinking of others. *(JOAN strikes a match.)* This violence is legal. It's every day. It's everywhere.

She tosses the match onto the gasoline. It sparkles and crackles. There is no flame... only beauty.

JOAN:
Ha! That's why science class is useful: you learn to mix apple juice with gunpowder and glitter... You're all stuck with me, until the end of the world.

Now can we please work together to make sure that end is as far away as possible? *(Silence.)* Yeah: this morning, I'd made up my mind to commit a radical act for radical times. But as soon as I opened my door, a mermaid – no, a siren – came out of the bushes and told me:

OLIVIER appears, dressed as a mermaid/siren: his tail forces him to take little tiny steps.

OLIVIER:
Joan Crust: I declare you necessary! When I think of you, it's not medals of crap that I want to give out: it's medals of thanks. Thanks for being the warning siren who keeps us from getting lost at sea. Thanks for having the courage to say "NO, I refuse," and for raising your voice when we need to hear but refuse to listen. Thank you above all for saying SCREW YOU, I'M ALREADY BEAUTIFUL. You're right. You are beautiful. In fact, you're magnificent. And I'm not trying to objectify you by saying that. This is not the patriarchy speaking through me. This is a human being who is lost and trying to find meaning in his life. That's what I want to tell you: you help me find meaning. Being with you is like reading *The Encyclopedia of Useless Facts:* it's good for me. If everyone was like you, the future would be astonishing.

JOAN:
Someone thought I was necessary. I, Joan Crust, was necessary. Crazy how the right few words, at the right moment, can wipe out a thousand wrong ones.

OLIVIER:
So then we came up with a new plan, together…

They exchange a knowing look and take their places.

JOAN:
(To the crowd.) Here's our plan: we've talked about the storm for long enough. Time to experience it. Ladies, gentlemen, and others: behold… the Barren Planet.

They begin to inflate a Barren Planet, creating a tableau – a sort of human graffiti, – in the image of their nightmare.

JOAN:
Can you see the problems with this planet? They're right here, staring us in the face. Global warming...

OLIVIER:
Political corruption…

JOAN:
Nuclear menace…

OLIVIER:
Migration crisis…

JOAN:
Xenophobia, homophobia, Islamophobia…

OLIVIER:
And the other ones that don't end in "phobia" but they're still scary anyway.

THE VOICE OF THE MAN IN A SUIT AND TIE:
Go on. Open it…

JOAN:
Yeah, I know: it's a lot.

THE VOICE OF THE MAN IN A SUIT AND TIE:
Tear... Destroy...

OLIVIER:
Enough to make you feel sick.

THE VOICE OF THE MAN IN A SUIT AND TIE:
Beauty never lasts...

JOAN:
But there's some good news. This Barren Planet is not just a menu of dangers.

THE VOICE OF A WITHERED OLD WOMAN:
Hurry… Please. Hurry…

JOAN:
This globe is also an all-you-can-eat buffet of resistance... a masterpiece where you can choose to say "no" to the masters.

THE VOICE OF ONE WHO IS HUNGRY, THIRSTY, HOT, HURTING:
I'm hungry. I'm thirsty. I'm hot. I hurt…

JOAN:
The good news is that EVERYBODY'S getting screwed, and "everybody" is a lot of bodies... enough bodies to make change.

THE VOICES:
Happy Doomsday to us...

JOAN:
The good news is that it's not true that IQs divide each other. The opposite is true: you, and you, and you, and you, and you, and me? We add up.

THE VOICES:
Happy Doomsday, Happy Doomsday, Happy Doomsday to us...

JOAN:
The good news is that we don't need to be the president, the principal, or anything other than who we are, to have power. The only thing we need to be, is together. SCREW YOU: THE ANTS OUTWEIGH YOU!

SOMEONE IN THE CROWD:
Shut up!

Silence.

SOMEONE ELSE IN THE CROWD:
We wanna dance. *(Silence.)* We just wanna dance.

Music: "Baby, Baby, Dance Floor." The crowd dances. End of the tempest... and of beauty. Very gradually, JOAN and OLIVIER give up, and start picking up the debris of the storm. We think it's the end...

Scene 12: Crap Medals

...but OLIVIER won't let it end there.

OLIVIER:
MEDALS OF CRAP!

(Realizing that the entire school is looking at him.) Uh... I... medals of crap.

I... award you a crap medal because your $5 T-shirt cost the life of three kids in Bangladesh.

I award you a crap medal because you think war is nothing but an action movie.

I award you a crap medal because you go around saying "I'm not a racist, BUT... I'm not a racist, BUT..." Well, I like everybody BUT I think you're a frigging idiot.

I award crap medals to the multibillionaires who, in the time I've been speaking, have made more money than I'll ever make in my entire life.

I award a crap medal to my neighbour who insists on learning the piano. It's been fifteen weeks and you still haven't learned "Twinkle, Twinkle, Little Star." YOU'LL NEVER BE MOZART. MOVE ON.

I award a crap medal to my Aunt Marie-Anne who's thrilled about global warming because – and I quote – "It'll be great for my tan." I don't think she gets it: nobody looks good when they're the colour of bacon. Same goes for the Earth.

I award a crap medal to the USA because down there, at sixteen, you're too young to drink or smoke or get a lottery ticket, but you can buy a gun at Walmart. That's okay, though, because we'll send our thoughts and prayers to the victims.

I award a crap medal to governments around the world who are starting to criminalize helping refugees. We're criminalizing compassion. I repeat: we're criminalizing compassion. What's next? Privatizing air?

I award a crap medal – one of the biggest, most beautiful crap medals I've got – to the entire educational system. A system which is based not on intelligence, but on memorization. Cram, exam, forget it as fast as you can. Why? BECAUSE YOU'LL NEVER USE IT AGAIN. Algebra? Please. Subjunctives? As if. The periodic table? Come on. You want to prepare us for the future? Teach us how to put on a gas mask. How to swim from ocean to ocean. How to revive a sixteen-year-old demonstrator who's been beaten by policemen armed like robots. IT'S NOT "MELLOW MIDDAYS" WE NEED, IT'S "MADHOUSE MIDDAYS." WE'RE GONNA BURN LIKE MARSHMALLOWS!!! DEATH, DEATH IS EVERYWHERE!!!

And my very last crap medal? I award it to myself, because in spite of all that, I will always keep believing that most of us are rooting for beauty to defeat despair.

Long silence.

JOAN:
There was no "Shut up." Or riots. No laughter. Or protests. Of course the crowd was gonna react. We just didn't know when. Or how.

Scene 13: The Weight of Ants

JOAN:
Olivier and I walk out of the gym. Away from the school. It's weird, but I feel... calm. Funny how comforting it is, not to be the only one yelling... I tell him: I have a plan. One last plan to finish up the week. A nice plan: not even criminal. We buy a big bouquet of flowers. We take the subway, the bus, and then another bus. When we reach our destination, we enter the building, we find the right room, and we open the door.

> JOAN:
> Hello Mrs. Principal's Mom…
>
> OLIVIER:
> Joan and Olivier. Pleased to meet you. We've come to spend some time with –

JOAN:
Lying on the bed is a woman who is breathing her final breaths. A body drifting away.

OLIVIER:
At her bedside, the principal, dressed as a sea lion, is crying his eyes out, holding his mother's hand. We obviously shouldn't be here. Just as we're leaving, we hear:

> THE PRINCIPAL:
> No. Stay. Stay.

JOAN:
We don't know what to do. We don't know what to say.

OLIVIER:
All we know is, the fact that we're here changes something. Maybe even everything.

They sit down beside the principal. A siren, a sea lion, and a match... silently bearing witness... to a mother's last breaths... drifting away...

Reflections for Students and Teachers
David Paquet

The Starting Point

"Resist." That is the first and only word that Théâtre Bluff suggests to me as a starting point. Right from the start, I tell myself: no politics, no youthful rebellion, no current issues. Too immediate and easy. So, I work on a first version, *Les angles morts* – "blind spots" – which invites us to resist hasty judgments and erroneous conclusions. Straightaway, I realize that the sections that are really landing are the ones that deal with... politics, youthful rebellion, and current issues.

Paradoxically, I choose *not to resist* what is emerging from the writing. A good decision: everything becomes clearer while writing the second draft, *Dans tes dents [In Your Teeth]*. By now, the piece has evolved into a political satire centring on a student election. Two teenagers learn to take the sorry state of the world in stride, and to bite – i.e., resist – so that they can keep on smiling.

But the end of that story is nihilistic. The characters seem doomed to change nothing, as if the play is the reflection of a widespread feeling of citizen impotence. That's not what I want to bring to the conversation. Especially not to young people.

Then comes the good version: *Le poids des fourmis [The Weight of Ants]*. Alongside social criticism and acid humour, empathy and solidarity emerge among the characters through a process of contagion. To understand the other is to offer them an invitation. This domino effect of people helping each other stand strong (or get back up) is at the core of the play. It's a reminder that beyond the weight that society puts on our backs, there is the weight that life puts under our feet. And there is what we choose to do with it.

Themes

When writing for the stage, one is advised to pick one subject – just one – and dive right in. Sorry: with *The Weight of Ants,* I'm not digging a furrow, I'm strafing the horizon. How – and why – should I talk about a single issue, when a multitude of problems demand our immediate attention? Or perhaps that's precisely the subject that encompasses them all: how do we resist when the threats seem to outnumber us?

> *Activism and Outrage:* Can a single person significantly change the world? If we think of Rosa Parks, Martin Luther King Jr, Emma Gonzalez, or Greta Thunberg, we have to answer, "Yes." The desire to have an impact on society is at the heart of *The Weight of Ants.* Running in a student election is a way for Joan and Olivier, our two protagonists, to combat their sense of civic powerlessness and give voice to their outrage. However, the election is orchestrated by an apathetic school principal who is devoted to the path of least resistance. The question then arises: is it possible to transform a system by following its rules, or does the solution lie in disobedience? *The Weight of Ants* oscillates, with humour and ferocity, between two poles: the desire for social change and the difficulty of achieving it.
>
> *Eco-anxiety:* In the play's second scene, an adolescent is offered the dying Earth as a gift while adults sing "Happy Doomsday" to him. In addition to tackling the urgency of the environmental issue head-on, the presence of eco-anxiety, in Olivier specifically, allows us to ask a number of subtle questions: does choosing to learn about the state of the world mean condemning ourselves to pessimism? Conversely, is optimism a form of denial? What is the consequence of lucidity: worry, or hope? Is it possible to find peace in the midst of revolt?

Solidarity and Engagement: At the heart of *The Weight of Ants* lies a simple yet fundamental mechanism: individuals influencing each other through their actions and words. Joan's nerve inspires the principal. The bookseller's mischievousness inspires Olivier, who in turn inspires Joan, and so on. This chain (re)action is a reminder that, despite our relentless individualism and thirst for personal gain, we remain connected and capable of mutual influence. "Society" is also the person right next to me. *The Weight of Ants* is a call to solidarity. Helping each other is contagious and galvanizing. In bringing together the smallest among us, we become heavyweights.

– David Paquet, October 2019